N. W. JERGINS

Wise Words Mom:

What to Say to Raise Kids Who Feel Accepted, Confident and Loved

For Clara and Andrew
Love, love. Love, love.

"My Mother is very well & finds great amusement in the glove-knitting; when this pair is finished, she means to knit another, & at present wants no other work."

Jane Austen

Contents

Foreword

You Are Powerful

A mother's words have incredible power. *Your* words have have incredible power. They have the power to give your children a **better life** by helping them feel more accepted, more confident and more loved.

5 Powerful Messages

In the five, short chapters that follow, you'll find the **exact words and phrases** you can say to convey **five powerful messages** to your children. These are not magic words, but they don't need to be, because they are born of something stronger than any magic—they are born of love, a mother's love.

Read on to see what wise words you can start saying, today.

1

Words That Help Children Feel Accepted

Message One: I accept that you are just a child.

"Take your time, no rush. I'll wait for you."

My son is tall for his age. His appearance says "teenager," while his actions scream, "Hey! I'm still a kid!" So he can fly like the wind when he's running the bases or chasing his sister, but his pace slows to a crawl when I ask him to grab his backpack, tie his shoes, and get into the car for the drive to school. In those moments of frustration, I remind myself that his executive function skills aren't fully developed, he's a lefty in a righty world, and he doesn't feel an adult sense of urgency because he's not an adult, *he's just a kid*.

Helping our children feel accepted starts with us accepting them—and their limitations—at their current developmental stage of life.

Imagine how our children feel when we rush them and expect them to move, act and learn at a pace beyond their abilities. We have an appointment to keep or carpool to drive, so we pressure them to: "Hurry! Move faster! Right now!"

I feel awful when I remember how I used to pressure my sweet daughter to get ready faster so that she could be on time for preschool. Her school day started at 8:30, but there was no real curriculum, just a loving teacher and bits of learning between lots of recess. Like the "good" mom I thought I should be, I made punctuality my top priority and rushed my daughter until she was in tears.

I had better options. I could have explained to the teacher'that, as long as it did not disrupt her class, we might arrive a little late some days. And, as I tried to teach my daughter the importance of arriving to school on time, I could have pinpointed the areas in our morning routine that slowed her down and adjusted those. Instead, I used "Hurry! Hurry! Hurry!" as my primary motivator, which only succeeded in adding to the stress-filled environment. I should have said some version of these stress-relieving, wise words to my darling daughter, **"Take your time, no rush. I'll wait for you."**

In hearing those words my daughter would have sensed my awareness of what she was currently capable of in life, and my acceptance of *who* she was in life—a child.

Message One: I accept that you are just a child.

What Moms Must Never Forget

In his book, *The Hurried Child,* author and psychologist Dr. David Elkind says it's important to realize that children do not need to be rushed in their day-to-day activities or in their mental or academic development. In one interview, Elkind explained what he calls the *hurried child syndrome*: "When a child is expected by his parents to perform well beyond his or her level of mental, social, or emotional capabilities...and ...behave and react as miniature adults."

I expected those very things from my daughter when she was barely four years old. At that time, I reasoned that if knowing how to read is a good thing, then knowing how to read at age four is a great thing! I bought a workbook with detailed instructions and easy-to-follow lesson plans for teaching young readers.

Precocious reading is fine, and some children develop the ability to read without instruction. But, in my case, I wanted to "hurry" my child along the path of learning, instead of acting on this truth: **children deserve a hurry-free childhood.**

We must not expect our children to mature directly from infancy to adulthood. There's a beautiful spot along that journey that we should acknowledge and embrace—childhood.

To fully accept our children, we should **make concessions** for their emotional immaturity, mental immaturity and physical

3

immaturity. I was reminded of this one day after firing off a to-do list to my preschooler. She looked at me with a defeated expression and said, "Mommy! I can't do all of that at the same time. I only have two hands. I'm not a caterpillar!"

Even my little daughter understood in that moment what I had failed to grasp—she could only do so much. She was not a miniature adult, she was a child. I should have given her a short, child-friendly list and said the wise words, "Take your time, no rush. I'll wait for you."

Turtles or Rabbits

The take-your-time mindset applies to older children, as well. So while we may realize that our children are not caterpillars, it helps to determine if they're turtles or rabbits.

I've written before about the benefits of identifying and accepting our children's innate pace. In my own home, I have one turtle and one rabbit. Once I stopped rushing my turtle, it made parenting less frustrating. If she overslept, I no longer expected her to get ready in ten minutes, and I learned it's futile to rush her out of her shell first thing in the morning. The wise words, "Take your time, no rush. I'll wait for you." brought more peace to our home, and I am sure, to my daughter's life.

In fact, just this morning, my son and I waited in the car for my daughter so that we could drive to school. I watched her walk out of the house and head over to my open window. With a note of distress she said, "Mom, where's my other uniform skirt?"

I wanted to tell her that I had no idea and that she needed to get in the car—now. I wanted to lecture her on why it's best to set out her school clothes the night before. But I knew that if I did she would feel pressured, and her day would get off to a bad start. Thankfully, we had a few minutes to spare so I said, "I think it might be in the laundry room." She immediately relaxed and said, "If you'll come back and get me after you've picked up the other carpool kids, I'll find it and meet you out front."

Thankfully, I tabled the teachable moment (another saying we repeat in our house is, don't try to teach someone to swim when they're drowning) and chose the better option: I accepted my turtle and allowed her to keep her day on track, and we weren't even late to school.

A personalized approach works for my rabbit too. Instead of getting onto him for rushing through homework or chores, I set up little systems to encourage him to be more thorough. I'll have him check off the steps of a project as he goes, so he doesn't blow past the details of what he needs to do. My husband will sit with him while he does his homework and remind him to check his work before he accelerates onto the next question.

The moral of this tortoise and hare story? Accept your turtle. Accept your rabbit. Adapt for both.

The Incredible Power of Patience

When we expect our children to function like adults, we set them up for feelings of exasperation and failure. We ask them to take their plate to the sink after they eat, and when they don't, we stare at the forgotten plate and groan, "You forgot *again*?" We teach them how to sort their laundry and get exasperated when we have to teach them the same lesson over and over. When we say to them, "How many times do I have to tell you the same thing?" It's as if we expect them to learn a lesson the first time we teach it. We don't expect that from a puppy, but we often expect it from our children.

When we **let our children live at their own pace**, *we* develop patience. I love the way author Susan Merrill describes patience in her book, *The Passionate Mom.* She says patience is "the ability to suppress restlessness or annoyance when confronted with delay."

As we develop increased patience in dealing with our children and allow our interactions with them to unfold at a childlike pace, we become calmer. When we are calm, we are more in the moment. We we are in the moment, we connect to our children minus the barriers of frustration or anger.

It is important for our children's sake for us to **accept the rhythms of childhood.** Doing so is the most effective way to relate to them, and the best way for them to experience life, love, and acceptance.

"Please, Mommy."

To help us parent with acceptance, I want to share a phrase that goes hand-in-hand with "take your time." Imagine your child saying the following phrase, especially when you feel impatient with him for moving slowly, not comprehending quickly or teetering on the verge of a meltdown: "Please, Mommy, be patient with me. **I am only a child**."

As mothers, we already know how quickly the time with our children flies. Why rush it? The beauty of accepting our children where they are is that we don't have to rush it; we can cherish it.

* * *

Message One: I accept that you are just a child.

"Take your time, no rush. I'll Wait for You."

2

Words of Ultimate Acceptance

Message Two: I accept you for being you.

"I am so glad that you are my..."

Wise words *can* change a child's life.

I heard a story about a shy little girl who attended a small, rural school. She came from a poor family and didn't dress as well as the other children, so they made fun of her, and she kept to herself. The girl's teacher felt sorry for her and tried to find ways to encourage her.

She found an opportunity during the students' annual hearing test. Back then, at such a remote school, there were no elaborate diagnostic devices for hearing evaluations, so the teachers had to improvise. They would call each child up individually and whisper a phrase into the child's ear. The student would attempt to repeat it, thereby indicating any hearing difficulties. Most of the time, the teacher would say something like: "The black cat climbed the mountain very quickly," or another generic phrase. But, when it was the discouraged little girl's turn, her teacher said something else.

The girl walked timidly to the teacher's desk. The teacher leaned in and whispered, "I wish I had a daughter just like you."

Tears filled the little girl's eyes. She repeated the words back to the teacher who rewarded her with a loving and kind smile. The teacher's words had gone into the child's heart and changed her life. Years later, the girl said that from that day forward she felt like she had value because someone had accepted her just as she was.

Message Two: I accept you for being you.

If a teacher's words of acceptance can have that kind of power, **imagine the power of a mother's words of acceptance**, words like these: I am so glad that you are my son. I am so glad that you are my daughter. I am so glad that you are my child. Those words show our children that we love them simply because they are our children. We love them as they are. They don't have to do anything or be anything to earn our acceptance.

Over the years that I've written for the motherhood site iMOM .com, I've read many parenting books. Among the most eye-opening was *Parenting at Its Best!* by Fred A. Hartley. Hartley says that when our children believe that we accept them as they are, their acceptance of themselves grows. Here is some of what Hartley wrote about showing our children acceptance:

Parenting begins with my **acceptance of who my child is**, not who I want him to be, not who I think he is, not who I think he should become. He may have my gender, my looks, even my name, but that may be as far as the similarity goes. That doesn't mean for a moment that he will share my ambitions, my personality, or my values. **Parenting begins with a big embrace for who my child is.**

The Gift of Acceptance

When I was growing up, my best friend was my opposite in almost every way. I had dark hair, she had light hair. I was fair, she was tan. I was shy, she was gregarious. Even though I knew my mother loved me, I could tell that she wished I were more like my friend.

"Why do you wear your hair like that?" my mother would ask. "Get outside and get some sun!" "Why don't you go to more parties?" I felt that I was not who she wanted me to be.

Years later, she apologized: "I am so, so sorry," she said. "You were so different from me that I didn't know what to do with you or how to treat you. Because I didn't understand you, I was afraid you wouldn't turn out okay unless I changed you."

The day my mother apologized, she gave me the gift of acceptance.

One of the most powerful things we can do as moms is to accept and celebrate our children for exactly who they are, to show them that we believe they are good enough, as-is.

My daughter loves horses. I am, for the most part, terrified of any large animal. But my fear does not squelch my joy in seeing my daughter's affinity for horses. I'm impressed that she's brave enough to get close to them, much less ride them. I praise her for how she treats horses with such kindness and self-assurance. And as long as I can stay at a safe distance, giddy-up!

I've learned to accept that my daughter will not share my taste in all things. I love vintage clothes, she doesn't. My decorating style is somewhat eclectic, hers is spare, with a modern flair. When I want to regale her with the study tips that got me through school, I back off (eventually), and acknowledge that her process sounds very well thought out.

We must never communicate a message that says: I wish you were different, and if you were different, I would fully accept you. Yes, we can offer encouragement and try to help our children improve in areas of weakness, but if they feel unaccepted for who they are, they will feel devastated.

I'll often tell my children, with an overly dramatic, tongue-in-cheek delivery, "I have the best daughter and son in the world!"

"Oh, Mom," they'll say, rolling their eyes, "Every mom thinks that."

"They might think it," I say, and then pause for effect, "But I *know* it!"

Even though our conversation is in jest, they know that I mean it. To me, I *do* have the best son and daughter in the world, and that's what every mom should believe.

Tell your children this week: "I am so glad that you are my son. I am so glad that you are my daughter. I am so glad that you are my child." With those words, you will plant a seed in their heart; a seed that will grow into a sense of security, love and acceptance.

* * *

Message Two: I accept you for being you.

"I am so glad that you're my…"

3

Words That Help Children Feel Confident

Message 3: I am always here for you—no matter what.

"You can tell me anything."

The growth of our children's confidence is directly related to their belief that we will always be there for them. That sense of security is the foundation upon which they build their self-confidence.

We see this when our babies look at us for reassurance as they take their first steps. We see this when our children look at us from the sports field for a "you've got this" thumbs up. We see it when our teenagers choose to tell us something difficult, because they are confident we will be there for them.

So, when we say to our children these wise words: "**You can tell me anything**," their confidence grows, rooted in the assurance that they have a safe place from which to navigate life. They live more confidently, knowing that if they stumble they can turn to us for love and support and we will help them figure out how to move forward.

This does not mean that we swoop in to rescue them every time they face a challenge, or that we allow them to escape the consequences of poor choices. But, ultimately, we do want our children to come to us and ask for help when they need it.

Message Three: I am always here for you—no matter what.

This is the true story about how the wise words "you can tell me anything" **saved the life** of my friend's 11-year-old daughter. Her case may be specific to the challenge she faced, but its broader lesson applies to all moms and their children.

The little girl, I'll call her Isabel, was in fifth grade and seemed to be happy in every way, but soon after her spring break from school she came down with a virus that took away her appetite. Days went by and Isabel didn't feel any better. She was listless. Her stomach ached, and she ate less and less.

Her mother Sarah took her to the pediatrician. "Isabel," the doctor said, "your stomach hurts?"

"Yes."

"Well," he said, "let's give it a couple of days. Since this has been going on for almost a week now, if it's a virus we should start seeing improvement very soon."

More days passed without improvement. The medical team ran tests and took X-rays. Sarah took Isabel back to the doctor and to the pediatric walk-in clinic. My friend was distraught.

"I didn't know what to do," she told me. "She was wasting

away, and the doctors couldn't pinpoint what was wrong. When I walked into her room in the morning, I was actually afraid that I'd find her dead."

That's when Sarah called her dear friend, Elizabeth. "I'm desperate, Elizabeth!" she sobbed. "There doesn't seem to be a reason for what's happening to Isabel."

Elizabeth **shared a phrase** with Sarah that would save Isabel's life. "Sarah," she said, "sit down with Isabel. Tell her, 'you can tell me anything.' If she doesn't open up right away, just keep saying it over and over."

"But, Elizabeth," Sarah said, "I've already asked her so many times if anything is wrong. She says no."

"Just say those *exact* **words**," Elizabeth said. "Trust me."

Later that day, Sarah and Isabel were sitting at the kitchen table. "You know, Isabel," Sarah said matter-of-factly, "you can tell me anything."

"No, I can't, Mom."

Sarah was surprised at Isabel's answer. "Of course, you can," she said.

Isabel went on to recount a story about her brother. "But, Mom, remember that time when you got upset after Ethan told you that he got in trouble at school for talking out in class? Remember? You got mad at him."

Sarah could see that Isabel was testing the waters, looking for assurance, event amid her doubt, that she could tell her mother anything.

"Yes, I was upset because Ethan's teacher had already talked to him about his behavior. But I didn't stay angry and I found a way to help him do better; remember? So do you understand? You can tell me anything."

And then, just as Elizabeth had predicted, Sarah's words broke through Isabel's resistance. "Well, I read in a science book at school that when you eat French fries, you only burn off a little bit of them and the rest stay in your body as fat."

Sarah now understood what was driving Isabel's stomach issues. Throughout the weeks of doctor visits and tests, no one had suggested that Isabel's problem could be psychological and biological, and if they had, Sarah would have brushed them off, believing that all was well in her child's home life and school life. And hadn't she asked Isabel repeatedly if anything was bothering her?

As Isabel opened up to her mother more and more, it became very clear that the phrase "**you can tell me anything**" saved Isabel's life.

Wise Words as Home Base

As I was working on this part of the book, I asked Elizabeth about the wise words she had shared with Sarah.

"**I learned from experience**," Elizabeth told me. "When my son was in his teens, he went through a rough time, doing things that were dangerous that could hurt him. Even though I didn't want him doing those things, and he knew it, I still wanted him to know that he could still come to me if he got into trouble. My message to him was this: **you can tell me anything**, any time of day or night. You can always tell me, and **we will work together to consider your options**."

When our children know that they can count on us, their confidence grows, and they feel secure enough to ask for help. We become their "home base."

A classic example of Elizabeth's philosophy in action is when a mom tells her teenagers not to drink or ride in a car with a driver who's been drinking. Of course, we don't want our children to drink, and if they do, we want them to know that there will be consequences. But, on the other hand, if they do drink, or if they're at a party we told them not to go to and all of their friends are drinking, we want them to be confident enough in our love for them to call us so they don't make a potentially fatal choice. How do we help our children overcome the fear of consequences so that they will tell us the truth? By being their "**home base**."

Four Ways to Be Our Children's Home Base and Get Them to Open Up

If we want our children to feel confident enough and safe enough to open up to us, we can try these four things:

1. Lay a foundation of acceptance.

As we talked about earlier, your child needs to know that you will always love him for who he is, regardless of what he does. Yes, you might be upset, but you will not stop accepting him and loving him. And while you may be disappointed with his choices, **you will not love him less**.

Dr. Nancy Darling, a researcher at Oberlin College, found that children are more willing to "...share information with parents who are warm." She also writes that children share the "most information with parents when they think their parents' actions are **motivated by love**."

If you have a child who's a people-pleaser, it's going to be tougher to get her to open up. She'd probably rather lie to you than admit she did something wrong or failed you in some way. How do I know that? Well, that's my mode of operation when it comes to messing up. I can't bear to disappoint someone I care about or respect. So if my friend asks, "Did you return that library book I loaned you?" and I haven't, I have to muster up courage to tell the truth.

We want our children to know that they can approach us with the confidence that **they will receive kindness and understanding** in their time of need. That's the loving reception we need to give them when they make themselves vulnerable to us.

2. Start early.

Begin planting the seed of "you can tell me anything" in your children's minds when they are very young. When you catch your toddler holding a marker and see the "decorated" wall behind her, say something like, "Oh, Ava, did you color on the wall?" If she shakes her head, try again. "Ava, it's OK to tell Mommy the truth. You can tell me anything, and I will still love you. I will still think that you are the sweetest little gingersnap ever!"

Yes, you'll want to teach your toddler that coloring on the wall is not OK, but more importantly, you want to start teaching her that if she opens up to you she can have confidence that you will respond with calmness, love and guidance.

As your child grows, you can go into more detail about your ground rules. "Sam, I want you to know that you can tell me anything. Even if you've done something wrong that I won't be happy about, it's better that I hear it from you than from someone else. Yes, there will be consequences, but they'll be lighter if you talk to me up front."

3. Stay calm.

When your child opens up to you; avoid overreacting. In her national survey of teens, researcher Shaunti Feldhahn found that 75 percent of them agreed with this statement: "If I knew my parents wouldn't freak out, I would really like to share certain things with them."

Shaunti writes, "Now here's the key: I was quite amused to hear kids define 'freaking out' as showing any emotions—even positive ones!" Kids want us to **listen calmly**, Shaunti says, without offering advice or launching directly into a lecture.

I know that's not always easy to do. There have been times when my children have opened up to me about opinions they hold, or something they've done that I didn't approve of, and I immediately went into lecture mode. When I did, my children shut down, and the sharing ended.

4. Provide hope.

Caretaking is my father's personality hallmark. He comes from a family of six children who are all witty and kind. One of my dad's younger brothers used that kindness and wit for decades as a child psychologist who specialized in counseling children who had survived trauma. He gave them hope by offering a vision of how things could get better.

He would tell them, "We will take all of those confusing feelings and fix them part by part, fear by fear, worry by worry, piece by piece." He gave them a plan, and with that plan, **he gave them hope**.

That's exactly what we can do when our children come to us after we have told them "you can tell me anything." We help them figure things out.

A friend of mine told me the tragic story of a young man, still in high school, whose girlfriend became pregnant. This boy was so ashamed that he killed himself. Soon after his death, his grieving parents bought an ad urging mothers and fathers to tell their children that there is no problem that cannot be brought to them and worked through.

The wise words "**you can tell me anything**" not only give our children a confident approach to life, they can also save their life.

* * *

Message Three: I am always here for you—no matter what.

"You can tell me anything."

4

Words That Help Children Feel Loved

Message Four: I will always love you—no matter what.

"Everyone makes mistakes. I still love you and believe in you."

I used to operate in the perfection-expectation mode; I unintentionally looked for what my children were dong wrong instead of what they were doing right. I especially fell into that habit with my son. All day long I would point out what he needed to do, re-do or not do. If I didn't reprimand him verbally, I would give him a look. During one of these correction-filled days, he turned to me with an expression of defeat, and a confidence level of zero. "What did I do wrong *now*?" he asked softly.

His words, and the dejected look on his face, jolted me. His expression seemed to say that he felt that not only were his mistakes unacceptable, *he* was unacceptable. **My constant**

correction had zapped his confidence and had probably made him wonder if he would lose my love if he continued to miss the mark.

So **beware the perfection-expectation mode of parenting**, and be aware of the other names it goes by: the high-expectations approach, the live-up-to-your-potential approach, and the be-your-best approach. Although it's okay for us to have high expectations for our children, and to want them to live up to their potential and strive to be their best, **it is harmful when those philosophies drive our parenting**.

Instead, continually reinforce that you love and believe in your child whether or not he's at his best or reaches his potential. Say these powerful and wise words to communicate that your love is not performance-dependent:

> *"Everyone makes mistakes. I still love you and believe in you."*

That message shows him that even in the midst of his failings you still love him; it's not the end of the world. We all make mistakes. Yes, we can teach him that actions have consequences, but be sure he knows that you still love him. Having that knowledge can make our children more confident and prevent them from becoming paralyzed by a fear of letting us down. Our children's feelings of acceptance and self-confidence grow when they feel secure in our love for them.

Message Four: I will always love you—no matter what.

We should not expect perfection. Our children should not be made to think that we will love them more if they do things perfectly or better. **Our love is not contingent upon their performance**. We must not expect perfection from them because they cannot deliver it. Even the highest-achieving child will not always find themselves in the top spot.

When we do expect perfection from our children we make them feel like they're walking on eggshells. "Don't mess up," they believe, "or Mom will get mad at me." Or worse: "If I mess up, Mom won't love me." They may not be able to articulate their thoughts, but that could be how they feel.

Most of our children's mistakes, knocking over their glass of milk for the third night in a row, receiving a bad test grade, or coming in a few minutes late after they've been out with friends, deserve a response that includes the message contained in these wise words: **"Everyone makes mistakes. I still love you and believe in you."**

That doesn't mean we ignore the mistakes, permit bad attitudes or allow our children to drift through life without boundaries or structure. It means that after all is said and done, we still love our children and believe in them, and we let them know it. That frees them to use our love as a solid foundation and live more confidently because they won't fear losing our approval. And, the more they act without the constraint of the fear of failure, the more confident they will grow.

Freedom from Fear

Author and parenting expert Dr. Scott Turansky compares raising a child to manufacturing a car.

"Parents are often frustrated by the continual need for correction and the endless number of mistakes that kids make," Turansky says. "If you can remember that your children are on the production line instead of in the showroom, your expectations will lead you to solutions instead of angry outbursts."

In this approach, the parent responds to weaknesses and unwanted "design flaws" by patiently regrouping. These parents understand that **their child is a work in progress**.

That kind of love is freeing and confidence-building because our children also hear this message: No matter what you do I will never *not* love you. Yes, we can express frustration when our children make bad decisions, but we need to say the words, "**Everyone makes mistakes. I still love you and believe in you.**"

What We All Need

I have made some big mistakes in my life. Mistakes I wish that I could undo. At those junctures, I needed to hear from those closest to me: "It's okay. Everyone makes mistakes. I still love you and believe in you." I needed reassurance that good could come out of my lessons learned the hard way. I needed hope and love to move forward.

Instead of expecting perfection from our children, let us **remember their fragile nature and their need to know that we believe in them and will always love them.**

* * *

Message Four: I will always love you—no matter what.

"Everyone makes mistakes. I still love you and believe in you. "

5

More Words That Help Children Feel Loved

Message 5: I love you enough to stand firm.

"I love you too much to let you..."

I remember the first time that I put the words, I love you too much to let you..., to use. My son wanted to stay up extra late on a school night to watch his favorite show. "I love you too much to let you stay up that late," I said, "because I know how important it is for you to be rested for school."

He stared at me, speechless, as he thought about which point he could successfully argue—my love for him, or the fact that he needed to be rested for school. The "love factor" had thrown him for a loop.

When we say to our children, "**I love you too much to let you...**" they understand, on some level, that we are are motivated by love, even if they think we are being "mean" or "unreasonable."

Our part in this approach is to use these words judiciously in situations where our love for our children and wanting what is best for them prohibits us from giving in.

Message Five: I love you enough to stand firm.

We can start using these wise words when our children are very young.

"I love you too much to let you play with brother's Legos. If you put one in your mouth it could hurt you."

In the elementary school years, we can say these words for character-shaping: "I love you too much to let you talk to me that way. I want you to to be respectful of others and learn how to control your words. So please try again."

When our children are **tweens or teens**, we go right back to the physical safety of the toddler years, and mix it with a dose of values sharing.

"I love you too much to let you go to Sasha's party. I've heard there's going to be drinking, and I know that Sasha's parents are out of town. It's not going to be a safe place for you to be."

These wise words are powerful because they do two things extremely well: they put our love for our children front and center, and they show our kids that we are willing to do what's best for them, even at the risk of them getting angry at us.

That type of response is echoed in Dr. Lisa Damour's suggested phrasing when teenagers ask to do something that you know is unsafe, "Nothing matters more to me than your safety," she says. "I don't hate fun. I love you."

***"I love you too much to to let you..." shows our children
we are motivated by love.***

Instead of: "Because I Said So"

In *The Sound of Music*, a father of seven, Captain von Trapp, barks
out orders to his children and demands immediate obedience
without any push back. Before I had kids, I imagined my future
children complying like the von Trapp children. I wanted to be a
"because I said so" mother and leave it at that. Once I became a
mom in real life, I learned that this expectation was not realistic
or healthy. Yes, there are situations when children need to do
what they're told without a drawn out negotiation. Dr. Damour
gives this example of a parent and four-year-old at clean-up
time:

"It's time to pick up your toys."

"I don't want to."

"Too bad. We can't do anything else fun until you do."

Dr. Damour says that children need us to provide structure and
boundaries. But **it's healthy for our children's development** to
let them engage in dialogue with us when we can.

Why Hows and Whys are OK

In the book, *Unequal Childhoods*, sociologist and author Annette
Lareau says that when children are allowed to dialogue with their
parents in a give-and-take discussion, they are **better prepared
to function successfully in the adult world**. But many parents
deny their children this option.

After I finished teaching a lesson to one of my seventh grade English classes, a student raised her hand to comment. "In my house," she said sadly, "I can't say anything back to my parents when they tell me to do something, or I get grounded."

Again, there are times when our children need to do what we say—pronto, no questions asked—but it's for our benefit, as well as for our children's, to let them share their thoughts. Otherwise, how will we know what they're thinking, feeling or believing?

This topic of dialoguing with our kids came up during a meeting with iMOM Director Susan Merrill.

"As a mom, I know it's tough to hear our children questioning our decisions and our values," she said. "But if we can stay calm and not get angry, their hows and whys will actually open the door for us to do even more teaching and guiding."

The Wise Appeal

Let's say that you've tried using the phrase, "I love you too much to let you..." and instead of responding calmly and respectfully, your child loses his temper, pouts, or says something like, "If you really loved me you'd let me!"

To prevent getting sucked into back-and-forth arguments, consider teaching your children Dr. Scott Turanksy's wise appeal—it's the perfect complement to *I love you too much to let you*. Dr. Turansky says once children learn the wise appeal "they're able to use it...both inside and outside the home."

Here's how it works: First, you make a request of your child. "Jack, your bedtime is at eight tonight because you have a big day at school tomorrow and then practice after that." Jack is not happy with your plan. Knowing how to use the wise appeal gives him an option other than having a meltdown. It also gives you an option other than, "Because I said so!"

Here are the four steps of the wise appeal:

1. **Your child repeats the request.** "You want me to go to bed at eight so that I won't be tired for school and practice." This teaches your child how to acknowledge your needs and lets you know he understands what's being asked of him.

2. **Your child shares his concerns.** "Mom, I don't want to go to bed that early because the big game comes on at eight. I really wanted to watch it." Knowing that he has a way to get his concerns heard helps your child stay calm.

3. **Your child offers a solution.** "So is it okay if I stay up until 8:30? I'll get all of my homework done, take my shower, and brush my teeth before 8 so I can go right to bed at 8:30."

4. **You respond.** If you agree with your child's solution, you can let him know or offer a further compromise. If you don't agree, make sure you've told your child in advance that a wise appeal doesn't guarantee that you'll change your mind. Part of having the privilege of using the wise appeal is being able to take no for an answer.

Another advantage of saying the wise words, "I love you too much to let you…"—is that they keep us calm too.

* * *

Message Five: I love you enough to stand firm.

"I love you too much to let you…"

6

Encouraging Words for You

Love, love. Love, love.

My daughter and son were born 21 months apart. When they were small, I would scoop them both up, one in each arm, and say, "My two beautiful babies." I would rock them side to side and coo, "Love, love. Love, love."

It all comes down to love.

Earlier in the book, I wrote that our words have the power to shape our children's lives because they are born of a mother's love.

That power isn't merely theoretical or limited to the content of our speech. Biological anthropologist Leslie Seltzer found that a mother's voice was just as effective as her hug in producing a stress-reducing hormone in her child. Stanford researchers found that, "Children's brains are far more engaged by their mother's voice than by voices of women they do not know."

A mother's words have incredible power. *Your* words have

incredible power. They can help you raise your children to feel accepted, confident and loved.

Thank you for sharing your time with me. I hope for you the same feelings of acceptance, confidence and love that you wish for your own children.

7

Suggested Reading

Here are some of the books mentioned in *Wise Word Mom*, and additional books that I have found helpful:

- *The Hurried Child*, by David Elkind
- *Parenting at Its Best*, by Fred Hartley
- *Unequal Childhoods*, by Annette Lareau
- *How to Talk so Kids Will Listen and Listen so Kids Will Talk*, by Adele Faber and Elaine Mazish
- *Untangled: Getting Teenage Girls Through the Seven Transitions into Adulthood*, by Lisa Damour, Ph.D.
- *Strong Mothers, Strong sons*, by Meg Meeker, M.D.

You can find my online parenting articles, here.

About the Author

Educator and journalist N. J. Jergins is the author of **Wise Words Mom: *What to Say to Raise Kids Who Feel Accepted, Confident and Loved***, an Amazon Top New Release in Motherhood, and an Amazon Top 50 Selection in One-Hour Reads.

Nancy is a Journalism graduate who worked on Capitol Hill in Washington, D.C., and spent many years as a TV news reporter. She returned to school to become a certified middle school and high school English teacher.

You can connect with me on:

🌐 https://www.imom.com/contributor/nancy-jergins

Made in the USA
Thornton, CO
02/23/24 16:06:05

a1cc28bd-40ea-4107-9240-de9e45941bd5R01